W9-CMB-320

Ornamentation in J. S. Bach's Organ Works

Da Capo Press Music Reprint Series

MUSIC EDITOR

BEA FRIEDLAND

Ph.D., City University of New York

This title was recommended for Da Capo reprint by
Frank D'Accone, *University of California at Los Angeles*

PUTNAM ALDRICH

Ornamentation in J. S. Bach's Organ Works

With a New Introduction by
ROSALYN TURECK

DA CAPO PRESS • NEW YORK

1978

Library of Congress Cataloging in Publication Data

Aldrich, Putnam.
    Ornamentation in J. S. Bach's organ works.

    (Da Capo Press music reprint series)
    Reprint of the 1950 ed. published by Coleman-
Ross, New York.
    1. Bach, Johann Sebastian, 1685-1750. Works,
organ. 2. Embellishment (Music) I. Tureck,
Rosalyn. II. Title.
ML410.B1A88 1978   786.6'092'4   78-17258
    ISBN 0-306-77590-5

This Da Capo Press edition of *Ornamentation in J. S. Bach's Organ Works*
is an unabridged republication of the edition published in New York
in 1950, and is reprinted by arrangement with Charles Scribner's Sons. It
contains a Foreword written especially for this edition by Rosalyn Tureck.

Published by Da Capo Press, Inc.
A Subsidiary of Plenum Publishing Corporation
227 West 17th Street, New York, N.Y. 10011

Foreword

Putnam Aldrich was among the first American scholars actively concerned with the art of embellishment. He made a major contribution in underscoring its indispensability. In recent decades this area of musical research has received increasing attention on the part of scholars, followed to a more limited extent by performers. Perhaps the sequence of interest is inevitable: historical practices are initially investigated by musicologists, whose discoveries subsequently become accessible to the performing musician. Performers sufficiently honest or curious to be interested in current scholarship may then acquaint themselves with the newest findings, and — ideally — alter their technique and their musical orientation in order to fulfill the music of a past era with historical authenticity and aesthetic validity.

Thus, the gap between the musicologist and the performer is at long last contracting. But more comprehension of historical data by the executant is to be desired, for the bridge of the fully-integrated artist-scholar remains shaky. With each new scholarly emphasis there tends to be an exaggerated application at the expense of the wider requirements of the art. This creates a new problem of specialized extremes. For example, "notes inégales" — as described by Quantz in his flute treatise — received widespread attention in the mid-twentieth century. Despite the fact that viewpoints regarding this practice remained unsettled and controversial, dotted rhythms became fashionable and were applied with comparatively little judgment and taste to Bach performance in large choral groups as well as to solo instrumental works. At present, in the latter part of our century, the informed performer (still too rare) is frequently seduced with the luxury of embellishment additions. The result is again unbalanced. Roulades of divisions are added, in repeats of variations, to a first playing which is often left bare. Thus we have an empty and sterile skeletal performance followed by the opposite extreme in the repeated section, where the music is choked with a honeysuckle growth of divisions. This lack of balance demonstrates the lamentable fact that historically correct devices are often applied unstylistically.

Putnam Aldrich was writing at a time when he felt it necessary to explain that "the *agréments* were by no means restricted to keyboard music" (pp. 10–11). He cites Michel de Pures, a seventeenth-century writer on music and theatre who attended performances at the French court.[1] In Aldrich's paraphrase, "trills and mordents executed by the singers, oboists and violinists at the court of Louis XIV were performed as evenly and as neatly as was possible on the best of keyboard instruments" (Aldrich, p. 11). The general comments on the appoggiatura constitute primary principles in the study of embellishment and provide an excellent foundation for a wider inquiry. These principles must be impressed upon the performer and teacher; they form the psychological and factual background from which a valid art of performance of seventeenth- and eighteenth-century music can emerge.

The sections devoted to the consideration of explicit symbols, although represented within the orbit of organ music, describe and explore broader historical and musical usage applicable to all performing media. The value of this book lies in Aldrich's understanding that the general guidelines of the vast art of embellishment, of the realization of individual symbols, including those *implied* for addition by the performer, are fundamental to the music rather than confined to specific performance media. Thus the realization of ornamental symbols becomes associated with firm musical principles, making Aldrich's work useful not only to organists but to all musicians who seek enlightenment in this field.

[1] Michel de Pures, *Idées des spectacles anciens et nouveaux* (Paris, 1668).

Aldrich considers a comparatively small number of embellishments, the primary types: trill, mordent, appoggiatura, doppelschlag, and a few "composite" ornaments. He does not pronounce absolute rules; he presents evidence based on original historical sources quotes musical examples where each type may be applied and, perhaps best of all, recommends legitimate *varieties* of treatment of these types. The book is not a vast compendium of symbols attached to varying national or individual notation-styles of seventeenth- and eighteenth-century composers. It conveys a sense of the general musical style in addition to illustrating the specific notational symbol.

Aldrich also understood that visual time values were not set down with arithmetic precision and on occasion did not necessarily represent the actual time value to be employed in performance:

> The formulas represented by the symbols were never completely stereotyped. Tables of *agréments* left by Bach and other musicians must be understood to be schematic rather than literal. That is, the *pitch* of the notes given in the realization of the signs is invariable in relation to the note upon which the sign is placed; but the *quantity* and the rhythmic interpretation of these notes was always left to the discretion of the performer. The schematic nature of these tables is readily demonstrated through a comparison of numerous tables prepared by different composers (both French and German). The melodic outline of each formula, as it appears in various tables, is identical but note values in which it is expressed differ with different musicians. Moreover, the number of notes in the formula is often incongruous with their time-values. Some writers deliberately used a notation in which no definite time-values are allotted to the notes forming the ornament (p. 12).

This point, still debated today, is of prime significance for understanding the psychology underlying the usage of embellishment symbols. To see embellishment notation as an exact orthography is to impose rigidity upon this florid art. The very essence of the musical psychology from which embellishment emerged and developed is non-arithmetical and non-precise, unlike the mechanistic frame of reference of the nineteenth century and the tyrannical categorization-processes of the twentieth. During these two centuries performance practice became less flexible, the composer's aesthetic expectations presumed to be altogether discernible from the printed page. This exactness binds the composition and its creator to one set formulation, diminishing the music's abstract character and thereby limiting its meaningfulness for future cultures.

An embellishment symbol involves every aspect of the musical composition. It does not apply solely to the melody, as is often mistakenly thought. Every embellishment sign is involved with every aspect of the structure — not only the melodic line, but also the harmonic situation, the rhythmic and motivic patterns, and the contrapuntal relationships that arise from the voice leading. Aldrich does not develop this point, and indeed it is too little recognized today as well. But he does perceive the wider implications inherent in even a single ornament symbol.

The chapter on the trill discusses the question of dissonance, so much a part of the embellishment function. The author touches a deeper level when he refers to the trill on a cadence — appearing as it so often does on the penultimate beat — as a necessary accessory to the *creation* of the cadence. The broader significance of this point, insufficiently stressed by Aldrich, is the vast part that embellishment plays in the structure of a composition. Embellishment is not, as too many today still view it, solely a device for filling out the music, although this view is at least an improvement upon the earlier one — namely, that embellishment is just a decoration without which the music may be satisfactorily fulfilled.[2]

The virtuoso decorative approach, although useful in individual applications, is not only a limited, and limiting, usage of embellishment realization. Its narrowness of concept and application endangers the compositional structure of music where structural relationships are so subtle and complex — as with J. S. Bach, whether in the organ works or those for other performing media. Only when embellishment as a more pervasive structural function enters the ken of all those involved in this indispensable art will the musical totality implicit in its study and practice be fulfilled.

[2] Ernest Hutcheson, *The Literature of the Piano*. third edition, rev. by Rudolph Ganz (New York: Knopf, 1972). In reference to embellishment symbols, Hutcheson writes (p. 55): "When in doubt, leave 'em out."

Aldrich's fundamental belief lies, no doubt, in the following quotation:

> The internal evidence of the music itself is a far better guide than that of more or less dubious sources (p. 14).

Scholarship must continuously uncover sources, selecting and sifting the best among them. The study of reliable sources must, however, ally itself with the evidence contained within the music itself. The latter requires intensive study and thought comparable to the arduous research of the musicologist. Ideally there is an integration of scholarly precision and inspired musical vision. In the end, the inner revelation must be fulfilled in performance by an endlessly cultivated subtlety of performing technique in order to articulate and project the formal as well as the spiritual qualities of the music with the greatest clarity.

ROSALYN TURECK
June 1978

Ornamentation in J. S. Bach's Organ Works

PUTNAM ALDRICH

Ornamentation in J. S. Bach's Organ Works

NEW YORK

COLEMAN-ROSS COMPANY · INC.

1950

CONTENTS

Table of Ornaments from J. S. Bach's
Clavierbüchlein vor Wilhelm Friedemann Bach (1770).

Introduction

'ORNAMENTATION,' writes Paul Henry Lang in his monumental study of music in western civilization, is 'the most typical feature of baroque style, equally prominent in all phases of baroque art.' [1] Musical ornamentation is no exception. It is now generally recognized that the ornaments form an integral part of the musical language of Bach's time, and that a performance of his works in which the trills, turns, appoggiaturas, and mordents are omitted or interpreted incorrectly, does violence to the musical ideas he intended to express. Organists who are conscientious musicians and devoted to Bach's works doubtless feel a sincere desire to carry out the composer's intentions. But they are often perplexed as to just how to proceed in order to do so, being handicapped at the start by a lack of reliable guides. Modern editions of Bach's works conflict with each other in regard to the signs and placing of the ornaments as well as in their directions for executing them. Efforts to solve the problem by consulting the works of scholars such as Pirro, Schweitzer, and Dannreuther only lead to further confusion: the experts disagree among themselves.

There are two reasons for these discrepancies and for the unreliability of editors and commentators: (1) these scholars base their interpretations upon documents that were written too late

---

[1] *Music in Western Civilization* (New York: W. W. Norton & Co., 1941), p. 359.

1

to be trustworthy guides to Bach's practice; (2) they undertake their quest for authenticity along the lines of 19th-century research, which are not applicable to the Baroque period.

Both Pirro[2] and Schweitzer[3] are guilty of lapses in scholarship when they base their discussions of Bach's ornaments upon directions given by Carl Philipp Emanuel Bach, Quantz, and Türk in treatises that were not published until *after* Bach's death. Dannreuther's treatment of Bach's ornamentation is marred by similar inconsistencies; after dealing competently with 17th-century ornamentation as exemplified in the works of Bach's forerunners, he proceeds, in the case of Bach himself, to adduce numerous exceptions to the common practice of the period—exceptions, needless to say, that Bach had never heard of—and to introduce, arbitrarily, new ornaments such as the so-called 'Pralltriller,' whose invention actually dates from the following generation.[4] Caspar Koch, the most recent contributor to the literature of this subject, falls into the same error that his predecessors did, by citing, in support of his directions, realizations of ornaments extracted from treatises by Marpurg (1750), Quantz (1752), C. P. E. Bach (1753), Leopold Mozart (1756), Dom Bedos de Celles (1778), Rellstab (1789), and Türk (1789).[5]

Now it so happens that the last half of the 18th century is precisely the period of the most rapid changes in both the composition and performance of music—changes which brought about the disintegration of the Baroque ideals and the formation of the Classic style of Mozart, Haydn, and Beethoven.[6] Interspersed with the conventions that carry over from Bach's lifetime are innumerable innovations presaging the new style. It becomes

[2] A. Pirro, *Johann Sebastian Bach, the Organist and His Works,* trans. W. Goodrich (New York: G. Schirmer, Inc., 1902).

[3] A. Schweitzer, *J. S. Bach* (Leipzig, 1911), and the Preface to the G. Schirmer Edition of Bach's Organ Works.

[4] E. Dannreuther, *Musical Ornamentation* (London: Novello, 1893-95), Vol. I, pp. 161-210.

[5] Caspar Koch, *The Organ Student's Gradus ad Parnassum* (New York: J. Fischer & Bro., 1945).

[6] Koch must be aware of this fact, since he writes (p. xi) : 'The somewhat violent shift in style and taste which marked the middle of the XVIII Century was a vital factor in obscuring for us the compositional and interpretive methods of the preceding era.' Yet, in his chapter on Ornamentation, he fails to take this into account.

difficult even to distinguish a single, unified common practice for this period. It would seem evident that there is no justification for assuming that its usage is similar to Bach's. Yet, with the exception of a short article by Wanda Landowska,[7] the present writer knows of no published commentary on Bach's ornaments that is based exclusively upon sources accessible to Bach himself.

Equally hazardous as the reliance upon anachronistic source materials is the use of methods of research which leave out of consideration the most important issue of all, namely, the fact that Baroque ideals of performance differed fundamentally from those of the present day. The problem, here, hinges primarily upon the attitude of the musician toward the printed or manuscript score. Nowadays, we regard the composer's manuscript as the final authority on any debatable point of interpretation. If we wish to obtain an authentic reading of a piece by Brahms, Schumann, or even Beethoven, we can find no better procedure than to consult the autograph manuscript and follow, note for note and sign for sign, the indications that the composer set down on paper. This is known as 'letting the music speak for itself.' Unfortunately, however, the music of the Baroque period cannot be induced to speak for itself. At that time the division of labor which has separated composition and performance into two distinct fields of specialization had not yet come into effect. All composers were performers and all performers were composers, at least to the extent that they were called upon to collaborate with the actual composer in the re-creation of any given composition. Many details of execution were not indicated on paper at all, but supplied extemporaneously by the performer.

It follows that the autograph score is *not* an authentic record of how the composer or anyone else performed the piece. The method of editorial research developed by 19th-century musicology consists chiefly in tracking down autograph manuscripts and first editions and preparing an 'Urtext' that contains only the notes and signs actually set down by the composer. This is the

---

[7] W. Landowska, 'Bach und die französische Klaviermusik,' *Bach-Jahrbuch* (1910). Cf. also the same author's chapter on Ornamentation in *Music of the Past* (New York: Alfred A. Knopf, 1926).

procedure followed by the editors of the Bach Gesellschaft edition. Such a method is obviously quite useless, from the performer's point of view, in a situation wherein a 'corrupt' score (with additions and alterations in handwritings other than the composer's) may be more authoritative than a 'pure' one, and no score can be completely authoritative.

The above remarks have shown that the inadequacies of most treatments of Bach's ornamentation stem from their failure to view the music in its proper historical perspective. Any successful attempt to recapture the letter and the spirit of Bach's music must consider it not as an isolated phenomenon but in its relationship to the music that preceded and followed it and in its relationship to the common musical practice of its own time. In other words, the historical approach is the only one that can hope to avoid misinterpretations that arise through the infiltration of ideals and concepts that belong to other epochs and styles.

The Historical Approach

In most respects Johann Sebastian Bach was a very conventional composer. During the early part of his career he never undertook to write in a form or style that was new to him without making a thorough preliminary study of what his predecessors and contemporaries had already done in that particular field. His first productions were frequently almost slavish imitations of his models; he was not averse to borrowing the very musical materials of other composers when he found it convenient to do so. If, during his lifetime, Bach was able to put, so to speak, the finishing touches to the traditional forms and styles—so completely, indeed, that further progress became impossible for his successors without branching out in new directions — this was accomplished not by introducing startling innovations but by realizing the full potentialities of the materials and procedures of composition already at hand.

In respect to the organ works in particular, Bach's indebtedness to Frescobaldi, Froberger, Böhm, Pachelbel, Buxtehude, Raison, de Grigny, d'Anglebert, François Couperin, Dieupart, etc., has been pointed out by Pirro,[8] Luedtke,[9] and other commentators. Considered individually, Bach's early compositions rarely rise above the level of those of his most gifted contemporaries.[10] But taken collectively, these works already reveal that remarkable power of assimilation which is probably the most important single ingredient of Bach's mature style. The chief difference between Bach's style and that of other composers is that his is not a style at all—it is a hundred styles. So penetrating was Bach's comprehension of the works of his predecessors and contemporaries (foreign as well as German) that he was able to extract and utilize the best elements of each, and to arrive at a synthesis of Baroque styles.

However platitudinous these remarks may seem to the well-versed musician, their obvious implication is acted upon all too seldom: namely, Bach's music should not be regarded as a preparation for the Mozart-Haydn period, but rather as a culmination of the various trends of the 17th century. Consequently, in order to understand it and to interpret it properly, one must approach it from the point of view of the 17th century.

Such an approach requires, of course, an acquaintance with 17th-century music—the music which Bach himself used as a pattern for his works, and from which he drew his inspiration. Equally essential for the modern composer is a knowledge of 17th-century methods and conventions of performance which were strikingly different from those of the present day.

It has already been pointed out that the performer of music, during the period under consideration, was almost invariably also a composer. This is particularly true in the case of organists and harpsichordists, whose duty it was, as directors of the 'Capella,' to furnish new music every week, as well as to improvise preludes and voluntaries and to realize figured basses at sight. Manuscript scores were written for use by the composer himself or his pupils and assistants. The comparatively few published scores

[8] Op. cit.

[9] H. Luedtke, 'Seb. Bachs Choralvorspiele,' *Bach-Jahrbuch* (1918).

[10] Cf. Pirro, op. cit., and Harvey Grace, *The Organ Works of Bach* (London: Novello, 1922) for analyses of Bach's organ works in chronological succession.

were destined for use by musicians who were familiar not only with the technique of improvisation and composition but also with the many more or less stereotyped musical formulas which constituted the common practice of the time. Is it any wonder that, considering the labor and expense of copying and publication, the composer should deem it unnecessary to write down every detail, when a mere hint or abbreviation would suffice to show the performer what was intended?

It was these circumstances which led to the adoption of those labor-saving devices which present interpretational problems to the modern musician and editor. The most obvious example of such devices is the figured-bass part which accompanied every piece of concerted music that appeared during the course of almost two centuries. It is now customary for editors to realize the figured-bass parts in their presentations of early music to the public. Their realizations are generally written in far too thick a texture, with inappropriate harmonies and other sylistic features entirely foreign to the period when the music was composed. But even the best printed realization is unsatisfactory, inasmuch as it leaves the performer no latitude to adjust his accompaniment to the resources at hand or to the acoustics of his particular church or hall. Truly faithful interpretations of this chamber music can only be achieved when the accompanist himself is able to follow the clues implicit in the original score.

17TH-CENTURY ORNAMENTATION

THE PROBLEM of ornamentation in early music is closely allied to that of accompaniment from a figured bass, in that it demands of the performer an awareness of the underlying harmony and a familiarity with the stylistic procedures of the period. The art of ornamentation was originally and primarily an art of improvisation. During the 16th and a great part of the 17th centuries, musical ornamentation was left almost entirely to the discretion of the performer. Recognition of this fact should not induce us to minimize its importance. On the contrary, it should force the modern musician to realize that the score, as it is handed down to us, is often no more than a skeleton of what the composer expected to hear, and that in order to understand the true nature of the music he must first make an effort to recapture those elements which are not present on paper.

At this point a word of warning must be interjected. The statement that ornamentation in the 16th and 17th centuries was largely left to the freedom and discretion of the individual often elicits the following response: 'If musicians of that time played the ornaments any way they wished, why shouldn't we follow suit and play whatever sounds best to us?' This reasoning is fallacious. One must not lose sight of the fact that the 'freedom and discretion' of a musician of the 17th century would necessarily take an entirely different turn than would the freedom and discretion of a romantic or modern musician. The performer was free to select from a wide stock of ornamental material the interpretation that seemed, according to his taste, the most appropriate to any given musical context. The material at his disposition, however, was not unlimited. It was confined within the bounds of the style in which he had been trained. Styles of improvisation varied from generation to generation in a manner that exactly parallels the variations in styles of written music. The performer who introduces into Baroque music whatever ornaments sound best to him *now* is basing his preferences upon a musical intuition that has been conditioned by the modern or 19th-century styles in which he has been trained. The result is inevitably a mixture of styles that violates the taste and spirit of both periods. It is as intolerable an aesthetic atrocity as would be the interpolation of a Wagnerian phrase into a Beethoven sonata. The principle of individual freedom in the interpretation of music of past periods must be approached with the greater precaution since the style as a whole must first be reconstructed. The nature of the limitations of the performer's freedom must be defined before it can legitimately be applied.

During the 17th century a distinction arose between the florid *coloratura* and *diminutions* derived from the Italian school and the more concise ornamental formulas that were characteristic of French music. The French ornaments (known collectively as *agréments*) gradually became stylized and, in the latter part of the century, a system of stenographic symbols was evolved, whereby the form and position of each ornament could be indicated in the score without writing it out in full.[11]

Both French and Italian types of ornamentation were adopted by German musicians. The Italian variety, being entirely improvisatory, cannot be definitely located in the scores. For information as to the technique of extemporizing these ornaments and the places in the music where it was considered appropriate to introduce them we are dependent upon theoretical treatises. The first German publication containing thorough instructions for singing 'in the Italian manner' is J. A. Herbst's *Musica prattica moderna*[12] which appeared in 1648. Increasing popularity of Italian methods of performance in Germany is shown by the number of instruction books published during the last half of the century for the use of instrumentalists as well as singers. There is no doubt that *coloratura* and *diminutions* were introduced not only in German performances of Italian music but also in the works of such composers as Schein, Tunder, Krieger, Weckmann, and Reinken.[13]

As a pupil of Frescobaldi, J. J. Froberger was thoroughly familiar with the Italian style of composition and performance. But after his trip to Paris, where he became intimately acquainted with Denis Gaultier, Chambonnières, and other court musicians, his music shows as much French influence as Italian. He made prolific use of *agréments* in his own playing, and if his scores do not reveal an abundance of signs for these ornaments it is only because he left France before the stenographic system had been fully developed.

After Froberger's death, G. Muffat, J. K. F. Fischer, and G.

[11] Mersenne (*Harmonie universelle*, Paris, 1636) was the first to propose symbols to indicate the various *agréments*. The signs suggested by him were not, however, adopted by composers and publishers. After several other unsuccessful attempts, the system of signs introduced by Chambonnières in his *Pièces de Clavessin* (1670) finally gained currency.

[12] This work is virtually a translation of Part II of the *Syntagma Musica* of Praetorius (published 1619).

[13] For further details on the distinction between the Italian and French styles of ornamentation see W. Landowska, *Music of the Past*, p. 136, and P. H. Lang, op. cit., pp. 359-362.

Böhm were the most enthusiastic partisans of the French *agré-ments.* The compositions of Muffat and Böhm were, in fact, considered more French than German. This is important for our study, since it may well have been Böhm's *Choralvorspiele* which first awakened Bach's interest in the French style and led him to investigate it at the source.

BACH'S USE OF ORNAMENTATION

BACH, as might be expected from what has been said above, made free use of both kinds of ornamentation, basing his style upon Italian models on the one hand and French models on the other. His attitude toward Italian coloratura was, however, unorthodox; he wrote out almost all the long, melodic diminutions in full, leaving none of the customary freedom to the performer. Bach was severely criticized for this practice; he was accused of blurring the harmonic and melodic outlines of his music and of making it very difficult to read.[14] There are, indeed, few places in which the rich texture of Bach's music allows room for extensive improvisation on the part of the performer.

What impulse moved Bach to disregard, in this respect, the conventions of his contemporaries? Was he skeptical of the German executants' ability to supplement his melodies with arabesques and *fioritures* that were rooted in the tradition of the Italian *bel canto?* Or was he simply unable to restrain the imperious genius that conceived these immense phrases, built up from little groups of notes but forming an ensemble of expressive and architectural grandeur? We can never know for certain. At any rate, it was Bach's custom to write out in full the florid melodies of the slow movements to his concertos and sonatas, the 14th and 25th *Goldberg Variations,* and many others which, had they been composed by Corelli, Marcello, or Handel, would have appeared in mere skeleton form. For a graphic illustration of the difference between Bach's notation of such movements and that of other

---

[14] Cf. Scheibe, *Der kritische Musicus,* No. 6 (May 14, 1737): 'All graces, all embellishments, everything that is ordinarily taken for granted in the method of performance, he [Bach] writes out in exact notes, which not only deprives his pieces of the beauty of harmony but makes the melody totally indistinct.'

composers of his time, the reader is referred to the pages of Wanda Landowska's *Music of the Past* in which that author has reconstructed the *Andante* of the *Italian Concerto* according to the prevailing notation of the period.[15]

In his treatment of the French *agréments* Bach was far more conventional. As was his custom, he went directly to the primary sources for his models. We know that he was acquainted with the works of Raison, Marchand, Nicholas de Grigny, Nivers, and d'Anglebert, and that he copied out pieces by Dieupart and Couperin as well as a table of ornaments and their interpretation.[16] Moreover, he left, in the *Clavierbüchlein vor Wilhelm Friedemann Bach,* an 'Explanation of divers signs showing how to play certain ornaments neatly' [17] which corresponds almost exactly to the tables furnished by the French *clavecinistes*.

GENERAL CHARACTER OF THE *Agréments*

BEFORE undertaking the analysis of the individual *agréments* used by Bach in his organ works, a few preliminary observations are necessary in order to dispel certain popular fallacies and to indicate the true nature of the ornaments:

1. The purpose of trills, mordents, and other embellishments was *not* to prolong the sonority produced by instruments that were incapable of sustaining tone, such as the harpsichord and spinet. The presence of the embellishments in organ compositions should be enough to discredit this fallacy, but some commentators have put it down to a confusion of keyboard styles on the part of the composers. (This, by the way, is an exceedingly dangerous point of view; close study will amost always show that the early composers knew what they were doing and why they were doing it.) Further evidence, however, is present in the fact that the *agréments* were by no means restricted to keyboard

[15] An admirable example of Bach's working out of ornamentation in the Italian style may be found in his Sonata for harpsichord solo (Steingräber Ed., Vol. 4) which is a transcription of a Trio-Sonata from Reinken's *Hortus Musicus*.

[16] Cf. Pirro, op. cit., p. 70.

[17] See frontispiece, reproduced from the original manuscript in the Yale School of Music Library.

music. Michel de Pures informs us that the trills and mordents executed by the singers, oboists, and violinists at the court of Louis XIV were performed as evenly and as neatly as was possible on the best of keyboard instruments.[18]

2. The fact that appoggiaturas (*ports de voix* and *coulés*) were written in tiny notes should not lead us to confuse them with the modern 'grace notes' and play them rapidly. The size of these notes has nothing to do with their rhythm. Their typographical differentiation from the other notes was intended merely to show that they do not belong to the harmony as it is expressed by the figured bass. In chamber music this distinction was necessary in order that the accompanist, who had only the solo part and the bass (figured or unfigured) to go by, should have no doubt as to what chord he was expected to play. With the dissonant notes appearing in small type the underlying harmony was obvious at a glance. Performers became accustomed to this harmonic clarity and resented the 'confusion' that resulted when nonharmonic notes were represented in type similar to that of the harmonic notes. The fact that Bach frequently wrote out appoggiaturas without using symbols or tiny notes is one basis for Scheibe's accusation that he 'confused his harmony and melody.'

3. The *agréments* are an essential element of the melodic line; their function was primarily an expressive one. Georg Muffat, one of the first composers to introduce this type of ornament into German instrumental music, writes as follows in the preface to his famous *Florilegium*:

Those who indiscreetly decry the *agréments* and ornaments of the French method, as if they obscured the melody or harmony and consisted only of trills, have certainly not examined this matter well, or else they have never heard performances by the true pupils of the school of the late M. de Lully but only by false imitators. For, on the other hand, those who have comprehended the nature, diversity, beauty, sublimity, true position and legitimate use of these ornaments, which are directly derived from the finest method of singing, have never, to this day, noticed anything in them which places the slightest obstacle in the way of the distinctness of the

[18] Michel de Pures, *Idées des spectacles anciens et nouveaux* (Paris, 1668), p. 274.

melody or the trueness of the harmony. On the contrary, they have found in them an abundance of everything which is capable of enriching and sweetening the music and of enlivening what might otherwise sound too simple, harsh, or languid.

The French singing teacher, Blanchet, is even more emphatic in his insistence upon the expressive function of the *agréments*:

The *agréments* are to song what figures of speech are to eloquence. By them the great orator moves the hearts of his listeners, leads them where he will and inspires them with all the passions in succession. The *agréments* produce the same results. If one gives some thought to their qualities of force, energy, sweetness, amenity and tenderness, one must admit that they are capable of stirring the soul profoundly, and that to remove this sort of ornament from music would be to take away the most beautiful part of its being.[19]

The precise musical nature of this expressiveness will be more easily comprehended when we come to analyze the form, position, and interpretation of the individual ornaments. It will suffice, here, to say that it is based upon two principles that are perennial in the history of musical expression: (1) emphasis upon the dissonance or introduction of additional dissonant notes, and (2) melodic accentuation of the penultimate strong beat of a phrase.

It must be confessed that most organists and pianists of the present day perform a mordent or a short trill with a nervous twitch that resembles the reaction to the sting of a bee more than it does the attempt to express a heartfelt emotion. Only through a full realization of the expressive qualities inherent in the *agréments* can the modern performer overcome that uneasiness and agitation which seizes him when he is confronted with the symbol of an ornament.

4. The formulas represented by the symbols were never completely stereotyped. Tables of *agréments* left by Bach and other musicians must be understood to be schematic rather than literal. That is, the *pitch* of the notes given in the realizations of the signs is invariable in relation to the note upon which the sign is placed; but the *quantity* and the rhythmic interpretation of these notes was always left to the discretion of the performer. The

---

[19] Blanchet, *L'Art ou les principes philosophiques du chant* (Paris, 1756).

schematic nature of these tables is readily demonstrated through a comparison of numerous tables prepared by different composers (both French and German). The melodic outline of each formula, as it appears in various tables, is identical, but the note-values in which it is expressed differ with different musicians. Moreover, the number of notes in the formula is often incongruous with their time-values.[20] Some writers deliberately used a notation in which no definite time-values are allotted to the notes forming the ornament.[21]

5. Signs for *agréments* that should be performed were sometimes omitted from the score. A trill or appoggiatura was invariably associated with certain more or less stereotyped melodic progressions that were characteristic of the French style. When Muffat, Böhm, Fischer, or Bach borrowed these progressions they sometimes included the sign for the ornament, but at other times they did not trouble to write it in, taking it for granted that the performer would recognize the formula and supply the necessary embellishment. These typical progressions are comparatively few in number, but the same ones occur over and over again in Bach's works. A musician who is familiar with the French style of the period should have no trouble spotting them at once, and should be able to insert the missing ornament at sight.

Unfortunately, no modern edition of Bach's organ works is completely reliable. Even the editors of the Bach Gesellschaft edition have made a practice of omitting those ornaments which do not occur in all, or at least in a majority, of the existing manuscripts of a given work. Other signs for *agréments* have been omitted on the pretext that they are not in Bach's handwriting. This is surely not a justifiable reason; there must be many instances in which Bach's pupils have added ornaments in places where they knew the master himself was accustomed to play them, or where, through their knowledge of Bach's style, they suspected him of having inadvertently left them out. At any rate, a familiarity with the stereotyped passages referred to above will

[20] Cf. Bach's own table in which, under 'Cadence,' four thirty-second notes are given as equivalent to the time of a quarter-note.

[21] Cf. Couperin's tables, reproduced in Dannreuther, op. cit., p. 100.

help to liberate the modern performer from his dependence upon unreliable editions. The internal evidence of the music itself is a far better guide than that of more or less dubious sources.

It should now be clear that a knowledge of the functions of the *agréments,* of the positions in which they generally appear in the music, and of the degree of liberty permitted in their execution will be more helpful to the student than would a set of rigid and dogmatic rules of interpretation. The element of taste can never be wholly ignored in an art which was originally completely improvisatory. But, taste must have something to go on— some standard which it can take as a point of departure. The present writer intends to divide Bach's ornaments into basic types, to analyze the function of each type, and to define the limits within which the 'discretion' of the performer may safely operate, according to criteria set up by contemporary authorities and by the style of the music itself. Examples of each type will be selected from Bach's organ works, but an enumeration of all the appearances of each ornament would clearly be superfluous; when the reader has grasped the characteristics of each type the interpretation of any particular case should offer no difficulty.

CHAPTER 1

The Trill

THE TRILL (called in French, *tremblement* or *cadence*) was considered the most expressive and essential of musical ornaments by the French musicians of the 17th century. According to Bacilly, 'everyone knows that the most considerable *agréments* in music are the *tremblements,* without which no song can be complete.' [1] 'If,' writes Mersenne, 'the other ornaments are the colors and shades of music, one may say that the *cadences* are its rays of light.' [2]

Many varieties of trill were distinguished from one another by the use of such qualifications as *cadence pleine, cadence liée, cadence appuyée, double cadence, double cadence battue,* etc. These terms indicate nothing more than slight differences in interpretation which depended upon the position of the trill in the music. An exposition of the innumerable subtleties and distinctions that are expounded in detail in contemporary French treatises would demand far more space than we have at our disposal. (The reader is referred to the author's *Principal Agréments of the 17th and 18th Centuries: A Study in Musical Ornamentation.*) But it will be necessary to differentiate between a few, at least, of the principal types of trill that were used by Bach, as they are associated with certain ready-made formulas derived from the French school of composition. Since the original terminology is too complex and equivocal to be serviceable here we shall refer

[1] *Remarques curieuses sur l'art de bien chanter* (Paris, 1668), p. 164.
[2] *Harmonie universelle* (Paris, 1636).

to such types as the *cadence trill,* the *passing trill,* the *tied trill,* etc., using adjectives that will be self-explanatory to the modern reader.

The most significant of these types is the cadence trill, which is the oldest of all the *agréments* and the source of many of the other ornaments. A brief glance at the evolution of this *agrément* will demonstrate the expressive function of the trill and show why it was given such an important place in all contemporary treatises on musical performance.

EVOLUTION OF THE CADENCE TRILL

ONE OF the basic expressive principles of music is that of emphasis of the penultimate—the heightened tension just before the repose on the final note. In the history of occidental music the manifestations of this principle may be divided, roughly, into three phases: (1) increased melodic activity on the penultimate syllable of the underlying text; (2) dissonance coinciding with rhythmic emphasis on the penultimate beat; (3) the combination of dissonance *and* increased melodic activity on the penultimate beat.

The first phase is shown clearly in the recitation sections of the Gregorian Mass and Offices, where most of the text is intoned on a single note, with fluctuations of the voice only at the beginning, at the *caesura* in the middle, and at the end.

The second phase may be observed in the vocal music of the 16th century. The very word, *cadence,* becomes synonymous with the suspended dissonance accompanying the close. Thomas Morley, in his *A Plaine and Easie Introduction to Practicall Musicke* (1597),[3] gives the following example (Example 1), which causes his pupil Philomathes to ask: 'I pray you, how do you make your last note saving two to stand in the harmonie, seeing that it is a discord?' and Morley answers: 'Discords mingled with concordes not onnlie are tollerable, but make the descant more pleasing if they be well taken. Moreover, there is no comming to a close, speciallie with a *Cadence* without a discord, and that most com-

---

[3] This entertaining and instructive book, written in the form of a dialogue, has been reprinted in facsimile by The Shakespeare Association (London, 1937).

monly a seventh bound in with a sixth when your plainsong descendeth, as it does in that example.' Philomathes: 'What do you tearme a *Cadence?*' Morley: 'A *Cadence* wee call that, when comming to a close, two notes are bound togither, and the following note descendeth.'

Ex 1   MORLEY

The importance of the dissonance in these cadences lies, of course, in the fact that it emphasizes the penultimate beat. It is expressive in spite of being a formula.   Morley writes, on another page of the same book: 'As I told you before, the best maner of closing is in *Cadence,*' and when his pupil objects: 'In *Cadence* there is little shift or varietie, and therefore it shoulde seeme not so often to be used, for avoiding tediousnesse,' he replies: 'I finde no better word to saie after a good praier, then *Amen,* nor no better close to set after a good peece of descant, then a *Cadence.*'

Ex. 2   PALESTRINA

The third phase of emphasis of the penultimate is exemplified in the ornamental resolution of the dissonance. This procedure contributed much to the grace and expressiveness of the vocal music of the 16th century; its typical form, as it was used by Palestrina, is illustrated in Example 2. In instrumental compositions the ornamental resolution attained a much higher degree of complexity and gradually became crystallized into two main types of cadence trill. The first, which we may call the *simple cadence trill,* consists entirely of alternations of the dissonance and its resolution (Example *3b*). It will be observed that the last note of the formula is the dissonance itself, which is at the same time an anticipation of the final note of the phrase. The second type, which may be termed *cadence trill with termination,* brings in the note below the resolution just before passing on to the next strong beat (Example *3c*). Many examples of these trills may be found in 16th-century instrumental transcriptions of vocal works.[4]

Ex. 3   ATTAIGNANT

These cadence formulas remain to form the basis of the most important *agrément* used by the French *clavecinistes* of the 17th century. So close was the association between trill and cadence that the words *tremblement* and *cadence* continue to be interchangeable in France until the latter part of the 18th century. The only distinctions between the 17th-century *agréments* and the earlier cadence formulas are that a greater rhythmic freedom of interpretation was now permitted and that the initial note could now be an appoggiatura as well as a suspension.

After 1607, when Chambonnières published the first table of ornaments in the preface to his *Pièces de clavessin,* cadence trills were no longer written out in notes; instead, they were indicated in the score by symbols—either a wavy line, $\sim\!\!\!\sim$, a *t,* or a *tr,* according to the individual composer. From now on the dissonance

---

[4] Cf. the *Deux livres d'orgue* and the *Treize motets,* edited by Pierre Attaingnant (reprinted by the Société Française de Musicologie).

itself, whether suspension or appoggiatura, is omitted from the written score. But Chambonnières' example shows clearly that it is still present in the music, for he explains that the *cadence* always begins with the note *above* the written note, and it is easy to observe that the written note is always the resolution of the cadential suspension or appoggiatura. Indeed, the whole orna-ment is, in reality, an amplified appoggiatura, and represents the highest development of that sort of musical expression which can be obtained through emphasis of the penultimate beat.

BACH'S USE OF THE CADENCE TRILL

BACH made constant use of both types of cadence trill (simple and with termination). His notation of the simple type is often more explicit that that of the majority of his French predecessors and contemporaries. Bach made a practice of writing out the final note of the formula, which had hitherto been left to the 'discretion' of the performer. This habit is extremely helpful to the modern student, for it makes Bach's formula for this cadence ornament much easier to identify. In 'writing out the last note— the note which forms the transition from the trill to the following strong beat—Bach was obliged to curtail the value of the note over which the sign for the ornament was placed. The inevitable result is a dotted rhythm at the end of the phrase. The simple cadence trill, then, can be identified in Bach's works by this formula: a dotted quarter-note followed by an eighth (or a dotted eighth-note followed by a sixteenth) in which the dotted note is the fifth or the third of the dominant chord, and the short note is the anticipation of the final note of the phrase. (Example 4). A sign for the trill (ᵚ, ᵚᵚ, *t,* or *tr,* indis-criminately) should be written over the dotted note. But, even if the sign is not there, *a trill should be played every time this formula appears.* The formula must, of course, occur at a cadence, which need not, however, be a perfect cadence; it may be a false or an interrupted cadence, and the formula may occur several times in close successions.[5]

[5] As in the subject of the C minor Fugue (Schirmer I, p. 6).

Ex. 4   BACH

In spite of the fact that he included a specific sign for the cadence trill with termination in his table of ornaments, Bach almost always writes out the termination in notes. The original seat of this *agrément* was the middle note of a melodic progression descending from mediant to tonic, and Bach frequently uses it in this position.[6] It later became customary, in French music, to insert this ornament each time a progression similar to that represented in Example 5 appeared in the music. Here again, Bach follows the example of the French composers, and uses the identical formula. In these cases it will be found that the harmony is either a cadence, a rising seventh,[7] or a passing six-four chord.[8]

Ex. 5

INTERPRETATION OF THE CADENCE TRILL

THE FOLLOWING points will be obvious from what has been said above: (1) the trill must be played on the beat; (2) it must begin with the note above the written note (in other words, with

---

[6] As in the second phase of the chorale in *Wachet auf, ruft uns die Stimme* (Peters VII, No. 57), measure 18.

[7] As in Ex. 9*b* and the Chorale-Prelude *O Lamm Gottes, unschuldig* (Peters VII, No. 48), m. 1.

[8] As in Trio super: *Nun komm', der Heiden Heiland* (Peters VII, No. 46), m. 17.

the upper auxiliary); (3) it should be played in such a way as to emphasize that initial note which is dissonant to the harmony (or implied harmony).[9]

Reference was made, in the Introduction, to the fact that all tables of ornaments are *schematic,* in that they indicate accurately the melodic contour of the ornament but *not* the number or time-value of the notes of which it is composed. Thus, although Bach's table shows a trill on a quarter-note composed of five thirty-second notes plus a dotted sixteenth, this combination of note-values is not the invariable constitution of all Bach trills. The rhythmic composition of the ornament was left to the taste of the individual performer.

Ex. 6

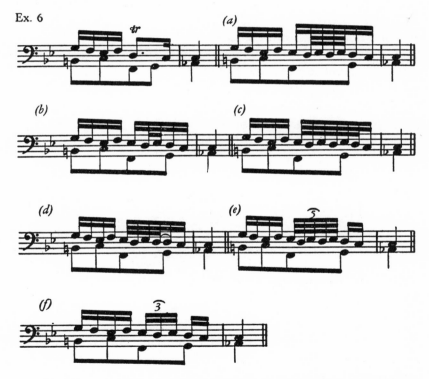

[9] It must be remembered that the cadential six-four chord was regarded as a double appoggiatura. Consequently, both the sixth and the fourth above a dominant bass must be treated as dissonant intervals.

Example 6 shows six possible interpretations of a simple cadence trill, all of which may be considered to be correct according to the traditions of Bach's time. The present writer offers
a few suggestions which may prove helpful in making a choice:
(*a*) is recommended for final cadences and pieces in a slow
tempo, where there is plenty of time to dwell upon the dissonance and still articulate the repercussions of the trill with
precision and clarity; (*b*) is good for particularly expressive
passages in a moderate tempo; (*c*) is especially useful when another voice is moving in rapid notes, for these can be co-ordi-
nated with the repetitions of the dissonance (cf. Example 7);
(*d*) is effective in quick tempi, provided that a note in another
voice is played at the moment of the tie; (*f*) combines gracefully
with triplet rhythms, but both (*e*) and (*f*) should be avoided
except where Bach himself uses uneven time-values. The advan-
tage of using an even number of notes in the trill itself (as in
c and *d*) is that the dissonant note with which it begins will then
recur upon each subdivision of the beat, thereby securing greater
emphasis. This principle should only be abandoned when it is
possible to obtain a still greater emphasis by dwelling on the
initial note, as in (*a*) and (*b*).

Ex. 7

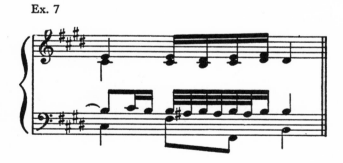

The interpretation of the cadence trill with termination is
almost always suggested by the note-values which Bach himself
indicates for the termination. In the third and fifth measures of
An Wasserflüssen Babylon, for instance, Bach evidently wants
trills of different speeds (Example 8). If, on rare occasions, the

trill resulting from this method of interpretation should be so slow as to cause confusion with the other voices, the note-values can be halved. But it is better to err on the side of deliberateness than on that of excessive speed; a trill which is not clearly articulated can never fulfill its purpose.

Ex. 8   (Peters Ed. VI, No. 12b, mm. 3—5)

Double cadence trills of both types are by no means rare in Bach's organ works. The one condition for their correct performance is that each trill should be played as though the other were absent. As such trills always occur at the interval of a third or sixth from one another, their beats will proceed in consonance throughout. A typical example is the opening measure of *Schmücke dich, o liebe Seele.*

The lists given below showing the positions of cadence trills in some of Bach's organ works will enable the reader to check up on his ability to recognize the specific types at sight.

Simple cadence trills indicated by signs in Volume One of the G. Schirmer Edition of Bach's Organ Works:

II   Fugue in C minor; mm. 4, 8, 12, 16, 20, 27.
III   Fugue in C minor on theme by Legrenzi; mm. 66, 70, 117.
VI   Fantasia in G major; mm. 15, 41, 46, 55. *Adagio;* m. 10. *Allegro;* m. 6.
VIII Fantasia in G major; penultimate measure.
X   Fugue in G major; mm. 41, 47.
XII   Fugue in G minor; mm. 9, 24, 51, 52, 54, 74.
XVI   Fantasia con Imitatione. *Imitatio;* m. 111.
XVII Fugue in B minor on theme by Corelli; mm. 34, 90, 101.

Simple cadence trills *not* indicated by signs in Volume One of the G. Schirmer Edition of Bach's Organ Works:

II   Fugue in C minor; m. 45.
III   Fugue in C minor on theme by Legrenzi; mm. 10, 18, 23, 26, 27, 46, 52, 81, 95, 104.
V   Toccata in E major (II) ; mm. 39, 55, 67, 71, 80, 81, 83, 88. Id. (IV) ; mm. 64, 93.
IX   Fugue in G major; m. 94.
X   Fugue in G major; last measure.
XIV   Prelude in A minor; m. 28. Fugue; m. 36.
XVI   Fantasia con Imitatione; m. 23. *Imitatio;* mm. 46, 98.
XVII Fugue in B minor on theme by Corelli; mm. 73, 77, 82, 83.

Cadence trills with termination from the Eighteen Chorales, Peters Edition:

Komm heiliger Geist, Herre Gott (Fantasia). Vol. VII, No. 36; mm. 89, 93.
Id. *(Alio Modo).* VII, No. 37; mm. 4, 9, 19, 28, etc.
An Wasserflüssen Babylon. VI, No. 12b; mm. 3, 5, 7, 9, 11, etc.
Schmücke dich, o liebe Seele. VII, No. 49; mm. 1, 2, 3, 4, 5, etc.
O Lamm Gottes unschuldig. VII, No. 48; mm. 1, 2, 6, 7.
Von Gott will ich nicht lassen. VII, No. 56; m. 1.
Nun komm', der Heiden Heiland. VII, No. 45; m. 27.
Id. *(Trio).* VII, No. 46; mm. 17, 24, 26.
Allein Gott in der Höh' sei Ehr. VI, No. 9; mm. 2, 10, 14, 22, 32.

The cadence trills that have been discussed thus far are immediately identifiable by the melodic and harmonic formulas in which they appear (Examples 9*a* and *b*). Bach does, however, sometimes use the trill at a cadence without introducing either of these melodic formulas (Examples 10*a* and 11*a*). At first sight this form of trill seems simpler than the other two, since neither termination nor anticipation of the following note appears in the score. Actually, this type of trill, indicated only by ⩕ or *tr,* is richer in possibilities, for it leaves more freedom of interpretation to the performer. The fact that the termination is not written out does not, by any means, prohibit its use. It was omitted from the score merely in order to give the performer the choice of continuing the trill throughout the whole time-value of the note, if he so desired. The permissible interpretations of this trill, then, include this possibility in addition to those previously illustrated for the other types of cadence trill.

Ex. 9

The most useful of these interpretations are given in Examples 10 and 11*b, c,* and *d.* It will be found that the trill with termination (*b*) is preferable for progressions where the note following the trill is identical with the upper auxiliary (as it is in Example 10).[10] In this way, any danger of the listener's mistaking a trill on B for a mordent on C is avoided.[11] The interpretation shown in Example 11*d,* on the other hand, is best where the melody descends one degree.[12]

---

[10] E.g., Trio super: *Allein Gott in der Höh' sei Ehr'* (Peters VI, No. 7), mm. 3 and 6; Trio Sonata I, *Allegro,* penultimate measure.

[11] As early as 1650, Jean Denis warned musicians not to use mordents and trills in such a way as to permit any doubt as to which were the principal notes of the melody.

[12] E.g., *O Mensch, bewein' dein Sünde gross* (*Orgelbüchlein,* No. 24), m. 3; Trio Sonata VI, *Vivace,* final cadence; the end of every phrase except the first two in the tenor voice of *Wachet auf* (Peters VII, No. 57).

Ex. 10

One of the chief requirements of a fugue subject is that it must establish a definite tonality. All fugue subjects, therefore, end with cadences, 'or with melodic progressions that may be interpreted as cadences. When these progressions pause on the leading tone or the supertonic just before the last note of the subject, they are invariably accompanied by a cadence trill. An examination of Bach's fugue subjects shows a marked preference for the type of trill that we have described above, for this position.[13] The reason for the preference is obvious: this trill allows

[13] G major Fugue (Schirmer I, No. IX); G major Fugue (Schirmer I, No. XI); C minor Fugue on theme by Legrenzi (Schirmer I, No. III); Wedge Fugue (Schirmer III, No. IX); F major Fugue (Schirmer IV, No. I); A major Fugue (Schirmer IV, No. V).

for an interpretation which varies during the course of the fugue, according to the voice-leading of the other parts. In many cases the performer will find that, while an interpretation of the trill as in Example 10*b* is most effective when the subject is first announced, the termination is best omitted (for the sake of clarity) in later entries.

Ex. 11

THE SHORT TRILL

IN TRACING the evolution of the trill we have seen that, from the beginning, its primary function has been to replace the appoggiatura or suspension as a means of introducing additional dissonant elements to the melodic line. Dissonance, from the 16th century on, has been closely associated with dominant harmony. The dominant seventh was the first dissonant chord to liberate itself from the laws of strict preparation. It is natural, therefore, that the trill—an essentially dissonant constituent of the music— should first have been used with dominant harmony, that is to say, at cadences. In the 17th century, however, dissonance was used more and more freely; appoggiaturas were introduced more and more frequently without the justification of cadential positions. Along with appoggiaturas came the trills, which, in Bach's time, were no longer restricted to cadences; in the French organ and harpsichord music of the period almost every measure bristles with them. The most common type of trill to be thus freely introduced is the short trill on an eighth- or sixteenth- note, which was inserted wherever an appoggiatura would have been appropriate, but where the composer desired heightened melodic activity as well as dissonance. One must not forget, however, that this heightened melodic activity is a secondary consideration, which must be subordinated to a clear presentation of the dissonance. An excessively rapid performance of the short trill defeats the main purpose of the ornament, especially on the organ, where the dissonant note cannot be emphasized except by a neat and rhythmic execution. The most satisfactory interpretation of the short trill consists of only four notes, played as evenly as possible (Example 12).

Ex. 12

The short trill, like the cadence trill, is indicated by either ᴧᴧ or *tr*, indiscriminately. Bach was inconsistent and careless in his use of symbols for ornaments; modern editors have been even more so. The position of the ornament in the music is our best

guide to its interpretation. The following are the places where
the short trill is most appropriate: (1) on the second of two repeated notes (especially when the second note is on a strong
beat);[14] (2) on the third of a chord, to fill out an arpeggio;[15] (3)
on either note of the interval of a descending second.[16]

A peculiarity of interpretation which sometimes occurs in this
last case has caused many writers to draw the erroneous conclu-
sion that the short trill should start with the main note. When the
trill is on a weak beat and the preceding note is itself an appoggiatura,[17] the first note of the trill may be tied to it, as shown in
Example 13. It is perfectly evident that this is no exception to
the rule that all trills must begin with the upper auxiliary. What
the composer has tried to express here is, of course, a trill on the
strong beat, with extreme emphasis on the dissonant note. In
order that there shall be no mistake about this emphasis, he indicates its appropriate duration in the notation.

Ex. 13

THE LONG TRILL

THE LONG TRILL is almost invariably found upon a note which is
common to a series of changing harmonies.[18] There is no difference in function here; since the upper auxiliary of the trill is dissonant to the first chord, it must be dissonant to them all. It
serves, then, to add harmonic interest to a succession of chords

[14] E.g., Trio Sonata III, *Andante,* mm. 51, 52, 54, 55, etc.
[15] E.g., *Wachet auf* (Peters VII, No. 57), m. 11.
[16] E.g., Trio Sonata II, *Vivace,* mm. 1, 2, 5, 7, etc.; Trio Sonata VI, *Vivace,*
m. 28.
[17] E.g., Trio Sonata IV, last movement, mm. 2, 4, etc.
[18] E.g., Trio Sonata II, last movement, mm. 75-76, 79-80; E minor Prelude
(Schirmer III, No. IX), mm. 19 and 20; E-flat major Prelude (Schirmer III,
No. VII), mm. 25 and 26.

which, being so closely related as to contain a common note, might otherwise sound a trifle dull. The trill should be continued throughout the whole value of the note, even though only indicated by ∿. The repercussions should be measured, so that the dissonance will coincide with each successive chord as it occurs. The number of repercussions should depend upon the other voices. A safe rule would be to play the trill in notes whose time-value is half that of the most rapid accompanying voice.

Bach sometimes writes a series of long trills in step-wise progression.[19] The important thing to note about such a chain of trills is that its harmonic function takes precedence over the melodic line. The melodic interest of the passage presumably lies chiefly in the other voices. One should not hesitate after

Ex. 14

interpretation

[19] E.g., Trio Sonata II, *Vivace*, mm. 66-70; Trio Sonata III, *Andante*, mm. 16-18; Trio Sonata IV, *Andante*, m. 38.

finishing one trill to take the leap of a third in order to start the next one with its upper auxiliary.[20]

TRILLS IN FUGUE SUBJECTS

THE PROBLEM of whether a trill which appears in the first announcement of a fugue subject should be played at every entry of the subject and answer throughout the fugue, cannot be settled by any general rule. One cannot depend upon modern editions, even the best of which contain inconsistencies and errors.[21] Even Bach's own manuscripts cannot be trusted in this matter. The composer may perfectly well have assumed that, since the trill was incorporated in the subject when it was first presented, no one could be stupid enough to play it otherwise; hence, it was unnecessary to write in the sign at each entry during the course of the fugue. This is certainly the case in respect to some of the fugues for harpsichord. In the organ fugues, however, Bach frequently alters the subject himself. Such alterations invariably take place at the end of the subject. They most often affect the pedal entry of the subject or answer, and they generally occur when four or more voices are active simultaneously. The present writer offers the following recommendations, based upon the foregoing considerations and a careful study of the music itself:

1. If a trill (or other ornament) appears at the beginning or in the middle of a fugue subject, it is undoubtedly thematic, and must be played every time the subject or answer enters.[22]

2. If the trill comes at the end of the subject, it should be regarded as a cadence trill.[23] The function of the cadence trill is to bring in dissonance on the penultimate strong beat. Therefore, if, at a later entry of the subject, the other voices furnish dissonance at the cadence, the trill on the penultimate note of the subject becomes unnecessary, and may be omitted.

[20] Cf. Ex. 14.

[21] Cf. Schirmer III. The first quotation on p. xv of the Preface shows a trill on the D of the alto voice, m. 21. The corresponding measure of the *text* (p. 42) contains no trill.

[22] E.g., F minor Fugue (Schirmer IV, No. II), m. 2.

[23] Cf. fugue subjects cited in footnote 13.

3. In those instances where the trill is to be retained through-out the fugue, care must be taken not to play it any more rapidly, at its first appearance, than is consistent with a clear execution of the pedal entries.

Before leaving the subject of trills it may be well to offer a word of warning about interpretations advocated in the prefaces to modern editions of Bach's works. It is lamentable, but true, that most present-day editors make no attempt to look up original sources; they either placidly copy the mistakes of previous editors or they resort to what may be termed 'scholarship by intuition' (i.e., it sounds right to *them*, therefore it must *be* right).

Particularly regrettable is the case of the complete edition of Bach's organ works annotated by Marcel Dupré. In his preface to each volume Dupré includes explanations of the signs for or-naments. The sign for the short trill, ∿, which Dupré calls *mordent* [sic], he interprets as a very rapid oscillation, beginning with the main note. As a matter of fact, this latter ornament was introduced after Bach's death, and did not come into general use until after Hummel had published his famous *Anweisung zum Pianofortespiel* (1828). The truth is simpler than fiction; there are *no* exceptions, in Bach's music, to the rule that *the trill begins with the note above the written note.*

CHAPTER 2

The Mordent

THE ORNAMENT which consists of the alternation of a melody note with its lower neighbor was already known as the *mordent* in the first part of the 16th century.[1] The derivation of the word, from the Latin *mordere* (to bite) suggests that the ornament had an incisive function. Moreover, it appears from the earliest preserved description of the mordent,[2] and the way Buchner used it in his *Fundamentbuch,* that the rapid performance of the accessory note and its immediate cessation (while the main note was held) served to emphasize the initial impetus of the note, somewhat in the manner of an *acciaccatura*. Rhythmic accentuation, then, was the primary function of the mordent as it was used in the 16th-century organ and harpsichord tablatures.

While the mordent seems always to have been instrumental, rather than vocal, in character, its use was not entirely restricted to keyboard music. The same ornament is found, under the name of *martellement* (or *battement*) in the works of the lute-composers of the 17th century,[3] and its interpretation is elucidated by Mersenne in his *Harmonie universelle* (1636). Now, there is one intrinsic characteristic of the lute which has a strong

---

[1] Cf. C. Paesler's article in the *Viertel-jahrschrift für Musikwissenschaft*, Vol. V, p. 32.

[2] Cf. Preface to Buchner's *Fundamentbuch* (1551): 'Memineris igitur eas notas quae curvatas habent lineas vocari mordentes, ubi observandum semper duas ease simul tangendas, ea videlicet per lineam curvatum signatur medio digito, proxima vero inferiorque indice digito, qui tamen tremebundus mox est subducendus.'

[3] Nicolas Vallet, Jacques de Gallot, Denis and Jacques Gaultier.

bearing upon the interpretation of the ornament under consideration: the tone of the lute begins to die away immediately after the string is plucked. All contemporary authorities are agreed that, in the performance of the mordent upon the lute, the string is plucked but once, the repercussions of the accessory note being produced by the fingers of the left hand. The dynamic effect was, therefore, as shown in Example 15. It follows that the ornament must, inevitably, have been played on the beat, as otherwise the rhythm would have been hopelessly confused. The function of the mordent in this music was not to emphasize the initial attack (which is quite unnecessary in a tone produced by plucking a string) but to lend animation to long, held notes, and to vary the *timbre*.

Ex. 15   **Ex. 16**

The French organists and *clavecinistes* of the 17th century adopted the mordent from the contemporary lute music. In doing so, they modified its interpretation so that it would be more appropriate to their style of composition. In the first place, the speed of the repercussions was reduced. Chambonnières, d'Anglebert, and their successors recommended the use of nothing faster than sixteenth-notes for the execution of a mordent upon a quarter-note. The number of repercussions was made to depend on the length of the note; most of the tables prepared by the French composers give the following two interpretations, with the understanding that other note-values should receive corresponding treatment (Example 16). Thus, with the ornament taking up one half or two thirds of the value of the main note and with a performance far less rapid than heretofore, the mordent began to acquire a melodic significance it did not have in the earlier organ and lute tablatures. The French composers suggest that when a series of mordents occur in close succession, the number of repercussions should be varied, in order to avoid monotony in the melodic line. François Couperin uses from three to nine notes in his interpretation of mordents which have thematic value, and even more when they are used solely for the purpose of animating long notes. He insists, however, that the ornament should never take up the entire value of the note, and indicates the *point-d'arêt* (stopping place) with a star in his realizations.[4] The expressive possibilities of mordents are suggested by the fact that Couperin refers to them in some of his pieces, as *accents plaintifs*.[5]

BACH'S USE OF MORDENTS FULLY WRITTEN OUT

BACH, in his use of the mordent, does not adhere to any single, stereotyped interpretation; he seems, rather, to consider the ornament as an element of composition which is capable of taking on different aspects according to its context. It is perhaps due to this attitude that we find the mordent fully written out by Bach more frequently than we do in the works of any other composer. The analysis of a few examples of this sort will throw a great deal of light upon the functions of the mordent in various contexts, and at the same time furnish us with models for its interpretation in those places where Bach indicated it by sign alone:

Ex. 17

The *Adagio* of the C major Toccata[6] contains admirable illustrations of the expressive use of the mordent (Example 17). Bach obviously wrote out the mordents on G sharp and A in the third measure in order to forestall any tendency on the part of

[4] In his treatise *L'art de toucher le clavecin* (1717).
[5] E.g., 'Le rossignol en amour.'
[6] Schirmer II, No. IX.

the performer to hurry—an eventuality which would be disastrous to the expressive resolution of the Neapolitan/sixth.

Ex. 18

The mordent which appears in the *Allegro* of the C minor Trio Sonata (measures 69-70, etc.) may undoubtedly be regarded as thematic, occurring, as it does, several times in sequential passages (Example 18). Bach found the mordent figure invaluable as raw material for composition, and frequently based entire movements on it. The most obvious example of this is the first movement of the third Brandenburg Concerto—a veritable apotheosis of the mordent. The D minor Organ Prelude[7] is built upon a figure (Example 19a) which, had it been written by a Frenchman, would have been expressed as shown in Example 19b. The practice of incorporating mordents in his themes is by no means exceptional in Bach's works; the F major Toccata[8] is a case exactly analogous to the last one, and the subject of the A minor Fugue[9] contains the identical figure.

Ex. 19

Bach's use of the mordent to animate long, held notes in illustrated several times in the *Andante* of the D minor Trio Sonata. The reader will note that, by restricting the motion to an easy flow of sixteenth-notes, Bach avoids any *excessive* animation

[7] Schirmer III, No. VI.
[8] Peters III, No. 2.
[9] Schirmer I, No. XIV.

which might destroy the tranquil mood of the piece. For the sake
of variety, the mordent is twice interrupted by a tie (Example
20). In writing out another long mordent, in the C major Prelude,[10] Bach attains variety by doubling the pace for the last half
of the note's duration.

Ex. 20

Interpretation of Bach's Mordents

Having considered the manner in which Bach himself interpreted the mordent in those places where—much to the indignation of contemporary performers—he prescribes definite note-
values for its execution, we are in a much better position to
evaluate the possible interpretations of these mordents which the
composer indicated by signs.

Bach's sign for the mordent (✦) is identical with that of the
French organ and harpsichord composers. The fact that he did
not adopt the signs of his German predecessors (such as the two
parallel strokes with which Kuhnau indicates the mordent) con-
firms our assumption that Bach always preferred to go to French
sources for his models, wherever ornamentation was concerned.
As in the French pieces, the length of the main note may generally be taken as criterion for the number of repercussions in
the ornament. In a few cases, it is true, Bach has specified his
desire for a long (or 'double') mordent by extending the wavy
line (✦). But these instances are comparatively rare, and
usually denote exceptions to the general rule.[11]

The accessory note in the mordent (as in the trill) is almost
invariably the *diatonic* lower neighbor of the main note. Wherever Bach wishes a chromatic accessory, he follows the example
of his French predecessors by inserting an accidental just below
the sign (✦ ✦). The term *diatonic* must here be construed

[10] Peters IV, No. 1, m. 8.
[11] As in the first measure of Ex. 17, where Bach desired a longer mordent on the
shorter note.

Ex. 21

as referring to the *melodic* rather than the harmonic minor scale, except where the contrary is expressly indicated by the accidental.

In regard to the speed and number of repercussions, we have seen that Bach himself was careful to avoid all excess, and that he most often contrived to fit the mordent into the prevailing rhythm of the passage at hand. An extremely rapid execution of the ornament, then, is rather the exception than the rule, and should only be used where a vigorous incisive attack is appropriate to the piece. It is effective, for example, in energetic movements played with a heavy registration, or in pieces written in the style of the French Overture, as the E-flat major Prelude.[12] Where the mordent is used thematically, on the other hand, we shall be following Bach's own teachings if we adjust the ornament to the rhythmic pattern of the other voices, whenever we can do so without making the final note too short (Examples 21*a, b, c, d*).[13]

When two mordents occur in succession, variety may be sought by 'doubling' the second one, as in Example 22. [14] The element of taste must be taken into account, here, no less than in the performance of trills. No one could accuse a performer of being 'wrong' if he were to play these two mordents in the same way. Similarly, the executant would be quite justified in applying the principle of variation to the subject of the E minor Fugue (Example 21*d*) by doubling the second mordent.

Ex. 22

Played

<hr>

[12] Schirmer III, No. VII, m. 1.

[13] (*a*) C minor Prelude (Schirmer I, No. II), m. 1; (*b*) C major Prelude (Schirmer III, No. II), m. 2; (*c*) G major Fugue (Schirmer I, No. X), mm. 4 and 5; (*d*) E minor Fugue (Schirmer III, No. VIII), m. 1.

[14] Trio super: *Allein Gott* (Peters VI, No. 7).

A mordent tied to the preceding note[15] forms the exact inversion of the short trill tied to the preceding note (which was discussed in Chapter 1). It will be noted that the preceding note is invariably an appoggiatura from below, just as in the case of the trill it is invariably an appoggiatura from above. The performance is, of course, analogous.

In general, it may be said that the mordent, in Bach's music, has a melodic function more often than a rhythmic one; that a relatively slow execution is usually to be preferred to a rapid one; and that the performance of the ornament should be rhythmic, in the sense that it should be neatly fitted into the time of the measure.

It is useless to speak of the so-called 'inverted mordent' for the simple reason that no such thing existed at the time of Bach. This mythical ornament is the fabrication of a series of misguided, if well-meaning, editors; the sooner it is forgotten, the better.

Ex. 23

CHAPTER 3

The Appoggiatura
(Vorschlag)

IN HIS table of ornaments, on the third page of Friedemann's *Clavierbüchlein*, Bach includes the figure given in Example 23.

The little hooks, or inverted commas, represent, respectively, the diatonic appoggiaturas from below and the diatonic appoggiatura from above. These signs may be unfamiliar to many readers —even to those who have a fairly thorough acquaintance with Bach's scores. The reason for this unfamiliarity is not that Bach did not use the signs in question but that modern editors have made a practice of translating them into those tiny notes which are, today, a better known way of expressing the appoggiatura. Those who are interested in seeing for themselves Bach's notation may look at the Chorale-Prelude on *Allein Gott in der Höh' sei Ehr*[1]—a piece which represents such difficult problems in ornamentation that even the intrepid editors have deemed it wiser to leave it alone. Or, better still, turn to the Three-Part Invention in D major[2] wherein the little hooks are used in almost every conceivable position.[3] Note that Bach's intention was to place the little hook on the line or space of the note that is actually to be played as an appoggiatura. Occasionally, his pen slipped, and the exact position of the little hook on the staff is indeterminable. In such cases it will suffice to remember that the appoggiatura

---

[1] Peters VI, No. 9.

[2] Preferably in Vol. I of the Steingräber Edition of the *Klavierwerke*, p. 24.

[3] Here Bach uses double as well as single hooks. The second hook calls for a super-legato in performance; it does not occur anywhere in the organ works.

will be from above or from below, according to whether the melody approaches the principal note from above or below.

The first question that arises concerning the appoggiatura is whether it should be played on the beat or (as is the case with the modern 'grace note') just before the beat.[4] This may be settled at once and without qualifications. The primary function of the appoggiatura is to displace the tonic accent from a har-monic note to a nonharmonic note. One of the chief reasons for representing appoggiaturas by signs or tiny notes in the 17th century instead of incorporating them in the normal notation was that the fundamental harmony was thereby made obvious to the continuo player.[5] The tiny notes do not belong to that harmony. They are dissonances, and for that very reason they are entitled to receive the tonic accent. They must, therefore, always be played on the beat.

The only real problem in the interpretation of the appoggia-tura is that of its duration. We know that, since it begins on the beat, it must 'borrow' its time-value from that of the main note. The question remains: how much of the value of the main note should the appoggiatura take up? Philipp Emanuel Bach recog-nized the importance of this problem and solved it, so far as his own music is concerned, by using tiny notes which express the actual values of the appoggiaturas he intended.[6] The theore-ticians of the last half of the century—Quantz,[7] Marpurg,[8] Leo-pold Mozart,[9] Türk[10] —arrived at another solution by establishing fixed rules for the length of the appoggiatura in proportion to the value of the main note. Thus, they explain that the appoggia-tura should take half the value of a main note whose time-value

[4] So-called 'grace notes' in 19th-century and modern music are generally repre-sented by small notes with oblique strokes through their stems. In performance they take up no appreciable time, and do not displace the accent, which falls on the main note. These signs and the ornaments they express are anachronistic to Bach's music. Wherever such signs are found in Bach's works they may be put down to the ignorance of the editor.

[5] See Introduction, p. 11.

[6] *Versuch über die wahre Art, das Klavier zu spielen* (Berlin, 1753).

[7] *Versuch einer Anweisung die Flöte traversière zu spielen* (Berlin, 1752).

[8] *Die Kunst das Clavier zu spielen* (Berlin, 1750).

[9] *Gründliche Violinschule* (1756).

[10] *Klavierschule für Lehrer und Lernende* (1789).

is duple (eighth-note, quarter-note, half-note, etc.), and two
thirds of the value of a main note of triple time-value (dotted
note, a note tied to another of half its value, etc.).

Unfortunately, neither of these solutions applies directly to
the interpretation of J. S. Bach's appoggiaturas. Philipp Emanuel,
in true pioneer fashion, describes his own practices and innovations with the recommendation that other composers should
follow in his footsteps. Never, however, does he pretend to be
his father's interpreter, nor does he even evince much interest in
the masterpieces of the preceding generation. The other German
treatises were all published too late to be acceptable as authoritative for the works of J. S. Bach. It is well to be familiar with
the main rules outlined in the preceding paragraph, since they
undoubtedly hold good for Haydn, Mozart, and early Beethoven.
Even for the period of J. S. Bach it is safe to say that the general
tendency was towards allotting to the appoggiatura half the value
of simple notes and the greater part of the value of dotted notes.
But no definite rules had been formulated at this time, either in
Germany or France. The duration of the appoggiatura was understood to depend upon the individual case and upon the taste
of the performer. At any rate, we may be assured that in those
places where Bach has expressed appoggiaturas by means of little
notes, the time-values of these little notes are purely arbitrary
and have no bearing upon the actual duration of the appoggiaturas. Nor is there any distinction between those appoggiaturas
represented by little notes and those indicated by signs. The
only clues to the correct interpretation are to be found in the
way the ornaments are used in the music itself, and in the
writings of the French musicians of the early part of the century.

THE APPOGGIATURA FROM BELOW

THE CLOSE relationship between the appoggiatura (or suspension) from above and the trill has been pointed out in the chapter on the trill.[11] A similar relationship exists between the appoggiatura from below (called by French musicians the *port de voix*)

[11] See p. 19.

and the mordent. Example 24 shows that if the trill may be regarded as an ornamental resolution of the appoggiatura from above, the mordent (in one of the positions where it occurs most frequently) appears as an ornamental resolution of the appoggiatura from below. The form illustrated in Example 24*b* is the exact inversion of Example 24*a*. Moreover, their relative harmonic positions also correspond, the trill generally appearing on the dominant, the appoggiatura-mordent on the tonic chord. So intimate was the connection between the appoggiatura from below and mordent that, in the works of several French composers, the former never occurs except in conjunction with the latter; the *port de voix et pincé* is treated as a single ornament.[12] There is, however, one important distinction between the trill and the appoggiatura-mordent. The trill may be preceded by a note other than the second above, in which case the dissonance, its first note, is attacked without preparation. The appoggiatura from below, on the other hand, is always prepared. In other words, while the trill may begin with either an appoggiatura or a suspension, the appoggiatura from below is always, in effect, a suspension resolving upwards. The reason for this obviously lies in the laws of voice-leading of the period. The dissonance with an upward resolution was barely tolerated under any circumstances;[13] such a dissonance taken without preparation was out of the question.

Ex. 24

(a) Played (b) Played

[12] Clérambault, François Couperin, Daquin, and others.
[13] Tartini, in his *Traité des agréments de la musique,* declares that the appoggiatura from below is 'contraire à la nature de l'harmonie.' He is apparently unaware that it has been an important ingredient of French dramatic expression for at least half a century.

Bach uses the appoggiatura from below in conjunction with the mordent very frequently in his harpsichord pieces, where the stylistic influence of the French *clavecinistes* is strongest. In the organ works, the ornament is not common enough to present any serious problem of interpretation as long as one remembers that the appoggiatura should be slightly dwelt upon before the mordent is begun, and that both elements should be fitted into the rhythm of the measure if possible (see Example 25, from *Wenn wir in höchsten Nöthen sein*).[14]

Ex. 25

When Bach uses the appoggiatura from below in final cadences it is usually accompanied by one or more appoggiaturas from above; that is to say that a good portion of the penultimate chord is suspended (but nevertheless articulated) to the final measure (see Example 26).[15] Models for execution may be found in many places where Bach has incorporated these suspensions in the notation.[16]

Ex. 26

[14] No. 42 in the *Orgelbüchlein*.

[15] Cf. also Trio Sonata I in E flat, *Allegro*, last measure of first movement.

[16] E.g., Prelude in E flat (Schirmer III, No. VII), last measure; Fugue in C minor (Schirmer III, No. III), last measure.

The appoggiatura from below in the second measure of Example 27 occurs simultaneously with a mordent in another voice.[17] It seems to the present writer that the best interpretation, here, is one in which the resolution of the appoggiatura waits for the completion of the mordent, because: (1) in this way both ornaments can be heard distinctly; (2) the appoggiatura resolves directly from the dissonance, which would not be the case were it given the value of an eighth-note; and (3) it conforms with the prevalent tendency to give the appoggiatura two thirds of the value of a dotted note. The reader must be warned that in cases like this, where the ornament is thematic, the entire piece should be examined before adopting a specific interpretation, in order to be sure that it will be appropriate to the voice-leading at later entries of the theme.

Ex. 27

Played

THE APPOGGIATURA FROM ABOVE

THAT this ornament is far more common than its counterpart from below is undoubtedly due to the general acceptance of the principle that dissonances should be resolved downwards. Bach uses this form of appoggiatura freely without preparation. While he incorporates it in the rhythm of the measure more frequently than do most composers of his generation, the little hooks and tiny notes which call for appoggiaturas are by no means rare in his music. In our execution of them it is best to follow the practice of the French *clavecinistes* and give the appoggiatura half the

[17] First measure of the Fantasie in C minor (Schirmer III, No. IV).

value of the main note whenever the latter is a simple note (i.e., not dotted) of comparatively short duration. Instances of this treatment in respect to quarter-notes, eighth-notes, and sixteenth-notes are shown in Examples 27 and 28.

Ex. 28

It must be stated here that the expressive value of the appoggiatura on a short note is identical with that of the short trill; the two ornaments are, in a manner of speaking, synonymous. There is a possibility that Bach sometimes indicated the appoggiatura in preference to the trill on very short notes in order to insure a clearer execution. A comparison of certain passages suggests, however, the more likely hypothesis that the composer used these signs indiscriminately. For instance, in measures 1 and 2 of the

Lento of the E minor Trio Sonata (Example 28) Bach has placed signs for appoggiaturas. At the recurrence of the same theme in the dominant (measures 9 and 11 of the second section) both appoggiaturas are replaced by trills. This shows either: (1) that Bach didn't care which ornaments were played, or (2) that he wished the second occurrence of the theme to appear in a more highly ornamented guise. In either case, this passage and others like it[18] establish the expressive equivalence of the two ornaments. The performer should consequently feel quite justified in substituting a simple appoggiatura for a short trill wherever a perfectly clear execution of the latter may be difficult or impossible for him. Conversely, the executant should feel at liberty to ornament the resolution of an appoggiatura by transforming it into a trill whenever he believes that he can thereby make the ornament more expressive. These are matters in which the 'taste' and the 'discretion' of the 18th-century performer came into full play.

Where appoggiaturas occur on notes of uneven time-value, careful discrimination must be used in determining their proper duration. First of all, one must remember that the chief function of the appoggiatura is to accentuate a nonharmonic note. If the last appoggiatura shown in Example 28 were to be played as an eighth-note (instead of as a sixteenth-note) its purpose would be defeated, since the C, instead of sounding like an appoggiatura to E minor harmony, would suggest a Neapolitan sixth. An analogous case[19] appears in Example 29; if these appoggiaturas were played as eighth-notes, the dissonance of a second (in the first measure) and that of a seventh (in the second measure) would both disappear completely. In order to avoid errors of this nature, the performer should always be careful to resolve the appoggiatura *before* the harmony changes. So long as the harmony does not change, the appoggiatura may be held for two thirds of the value of the main note—sometimes even longer.

A rather specialized form of appoggiatura used by the French in both vocal and instrumental music deserves mention here, if

---

[18] Cf. *Wachet auf* (Peters VII, No. 57), in which the sign for the appoggiatura and the abbreviation *tr* are applied indiscriminately to the same melodic figure.

[19] From the Prelude in B minor (Peters II, No. 10), m. 1.

only because Bach's inclusion of it in a few pieces proves con-
clusively that he was familiar with subtle details of the French
style. In performing a succession of descending thirds, the French

Ex. 29

executant, whether singer or instrumentalist, was accustomed to
fill in the intermediate intervals, in such a way, however, as to
'insist upon the sounds of the middle notes, but at the same time
slide over them quickly, tenderly and caressingly.'[20] When this
form of ornamentation (generally referred to as *couler les tierces*)
was indicated in the score, the sign of the appoggiatura was used.
More often there was no written indication; the introduction of
the ornament was left to the discretion of the performer.[21] The
appoggiaturas in Bach's *Allein Gott in der Höh' sei Ehr*[22] are
evidently derived from this French tradition (see Example 30).

Ex. 30

[20] Cf. Corrette, *Le parfait maître à chanter;* Montéclair, *Principes de musique;*
and the anonymous treatise called *La belle Vielleuse.*
[21] Montéclair states that descending thirds should always be 'coulées' except
when the movement is too rapid and where the text expresses anger or indignation.
[22] Peters VI, No. 9.

There is no authority for the exact duration of the appoggiaturas here; the interpretation given in Example 31 is merely a suggestion. There should, however, be some sort of distinction between the first three appoggiaturas and the fourth, which has no

Ex. 31

connection with the descending thirds. A further example of *tierces coulées* will be found in *Meine Seele erhebt den Herren.*[23]

THE DOUBLE APPOGGIATURA FROM BELOW *(Schleifer)*

THE DOUBLE APPOGGIATURA, consisting of two notes which approach the main note from the interval of a third below, is extremely common in Bach's music. Its proper symbol is the one shown in Example 31. The wavy line should be placed on the line or space belonging to the third below the main note. Bach sometimes misplaced it, just as he did the sign for the simple appoggiatura; such slips of the pen should be disregarded. Sometimes Bach used two tiny notes slurred to the main note to express this ornament. In many other cases, editors have replaced the sign by tiny notes. At any rate, there should be no difficulty whatever in interpreting this ornament, since Bach himself has shown us time and time again how it should be played, by writing it out in the ordinary notation.[24] The first two notes (i.e., the two appoggiaturas) are of equal length; together, they normally occupy the first half of the main note's written time-value. (See Example 31 and, for triple rhythms, the interpretation given in the first measure of Example 28.)

[23] Peters VII, No. 42, m. 23.
[24] Prelude in B minor (Peters II, No. 10), m. 49; Trio Sonata I, *Vivace,* m. 1, etc.; Trio Sonata VI, *Lento,* mm. 9, 10, etc.; *Wachet auf* (Peters VII, No. 57), m. 1.

CHAPTER 4

The Turn

(Doppelschlag)

THE TURN, as it is used by Bach, consists of four notes only. As shown in Example 32, it begins with an appoggiatura above the main note, passes through the main note to the lower accessory, and returns to finish upon the main note itself. It may be construed as an appoggiatura from above, followed by a mordent. Combining, within a very short space, the expressive, dissonant element of the former with the melodic function of the latter ornament, the turn is one of the most forceful and at the same time the most concise of the *agréments*. The four notes of the turn are generally to be played in an even rhythm—four sixteenth-notes for a turn on a quarter-note, four thirty-second notes for a turn on an eighth-note, as the case may be.

When Bach desires an unconventional rhythmic interpretation, or when he wishes the first note to be tied to the preceding note, he writes out the turn in the ordinary notation.[1] In Example 32*d*[2] the rhythm of the turn, as it is indicated by Bach, illustrates the relationship of this ornament with the appoggiatura and mordent. When the sign for the turn is placed between two notes, the ornament should be played in the second half of the time-value of the first note; consequently, it must be played twice as fast. Bach does not place a turn in this position unless there

---

[1] E.g., Sonata IV, *Vivace,* m. 7; Sonata VI, *Lento,* m. 2; *Mit Fried und Freud' ich fahr' dahin* (Peters V, No. 41), m. 3, alto voice; B minor Fugue (Schirmer I, No. XVII), m. 8.

[2] From the *Largo* of Trio Sonata V, m. 2.

is good reason to do so, for instance, to leave room for a mordent during the first half of the duration of the main note.[3]

Ex. 32

In the case of dotted notes, the placing of the sign over the dot does not mean that the ornament should be played in the time of the dot, but rather that the last note of the turn should coincide with the dot, so that the whole figure will end with two notes of equal value. Example 32 illustrates the correct interpretation of the turn in each of its possible positions.[4]

The reader may have observed that the four notes which constitute the turn are, in their relationship to the main note, identical with the last four notes of the trill with termination, which was discussed in Chapter 1. The fact is that all the essential elements of this trill (if one remembers that the successive repercussions of the trill are nothing but an amplification of the initial appoggiatura) are contained in the turn. The trill with termination and the turn may then be regarded as functionally synony-

[3] See Ex. 8, from *Komm', heiliger Geist* (Peters VII, No. 37), m. 15.
[4] Examples in Bach's works of the turn on a plain note: *Allein Gott in der Höh'* (Peters VI, No. 9), mm. 2, 4, 9, etc.; Duetto I, penultimate measure; Duetto II, 6th measure before double bar (in Part III of the *Klavierübung*). For the turn on a dot, see *Komm', heiliger Geist*, m. 36; *Schmücke dich* (Peters VII, No. 49), m. 33 after double bar.

mous, just as the plain trill and the appoggiatura from above are synonymous.[5] If we examine the places where Bach has indicated a turn over a plain (i.e., not dotted) note, we will find that they are musically analogous to those places where he uses a trill with termination.[6]

A comparison of various manuscript sources of Bach's organ works reveals the fact that the copyists often vacillated between the sign for the turn and the sign for the trill in corresponding phrases of the same piece, and that what is indicated as a turn in one copy frequently appears as a trill in another.[7] These considerations, together with Bach's own carelessness with regard to the signs of the *agréments,* suffice to justify the performer's substitution of a turn for a trill with termination wherever the former seems more suitable to the tempo. The player need only remember that such substitutions should not change the time-value of the written termination. In other words, the substitution may be made when the notes forming the termination have half the value of the main note,[8] but not when they are given only one fourth its value.[9]

It will be found that when the turn appears over a dot or between two notes there will almost always be some sort of trill on the *following* note.[10] The function of the turn, in such cases, is, in part, a transitional one; it serves to join the preceding note with the following note and at the same time to prepare for the more elaborate second ornament. A turn of this sort is always appropriate when a trill on a quarter-note is preceded by a dotted eighth and sixteenth; it may be introduced by the player in such places, even where it is not indicated in the score.

---

[5] This relationship was pointed out in Chapter 3.

[6] See examples cited in footnote 4.

[7] No hint of these discrepancies appears in any modern edition — even that of the Bach Gesellschaft treats them summarily. It is high time that someone should offer to the public a critical edition of Bach's organ works. Until this is done, we are at the mercy of purely arbitrary decisions between many equally authentic sources.

[8] E.g., *Christum, wir sollen loben schon (Orgelbüchlein),* mm. 2 and 3; *Allein Gott* (Peters VI, No. 9), mm. 2, 4, 5, 6, etc.

[9] E.g., *An Wasserflüssen Babylon* (Peters VI, No. 12b), mm. 3, 5.

[10] E.g., *Schmücke dich,* second edition, m. 33.

CHAPTER 5

Composite
Ornaments

ALL OF Bach's ornaments that have not hitherto been discussed may be regarded as composite—that is, they are made up of a series of simple elements. Such ornaments can most conveniently be considered in pairs, as follows:

APPOGGIATURA AND TRILL

EVERY trill begins with an appoggiatura. It may, then, seem redundant to speak of a composite ornament as an *appoggiatura and trill,* and it would be so in fact were it not that Bach sometimes uses a specific sign to indicate that the initial appoggiatura is to be held longer than its customary duration. This sign and its approximate realization are given in Example 33. That it does not occur very often in modern printed editions of Bach's works is partially due to difficulty with which it is distinguishable from the ordinary sign for the trill in manuscript sources. The reader will find examples of the sign in the Chorale-Prelude on *Komm, heiliger Geist, Herre Gott,*[1] and in *An Wasserflüssen Babylon.*[2]

TRILL AND MORDENT

BACH combines the trill and the mordent in two different ways: first, by superimposing the trill upon the first note of the mor-

---

[1] Peters VII, No. 37, m. 17. The same sign should appear in m. 2. See Ex. 39.
[2] Peters VI, No. 12b, mm. 8 and 20.

dent; second, by adding the mordent to the end of the trill. The first combination has no specific sign; the mordent is always written out in notes, and the trill is always a short one. There are no difficulties of interpretation here. The four short notes of the trill merely replace the first note of the mordent, as shown in Example 34, so that the rhythmic basis of the mordent remains unchanged. Bach had a great predilection for this ornament; countless examples of it may be found scattered throughout his works.[3] If the tempo is too rapid for a clear execution of all the notes, a simple appoggiatura may be substituted for the trill (as Bach occasionally does himself)[4] without altering the expressive value of the ornament.

Ex. 33   Ex. 34

The second way of combining trill and mordent results, of course, in a trill with termination. Bach's sign for this ornament

Ex. 35

(which appears in his table under the name of *Trillo und Mordant*) is only one of the many ways of expressing this variety

---

[3] E.g., Sonata III, *Andante,* m. 1; id. second section, mm. 9 and 11; Sonata VI, *Lento,* second section, m. 11; Pastorale, m. 2; Fantasia super: *Nun komm', der Heiden Heiland* (Peters VII, No. 45), mm. 15, 24, 29, etc.

[4] Cf. Sonata VI, *Lento,* m. 3.

of trill, whose function and interpretation have already been discussed in Chapter 1. Nothing more need be said here except a word of warning to the reader not to confuse this sign (see Example 35) with that for the long mordent, which always has the vertical stroke in the middle or at the beginning of the wavy line.[5]

TURN AND TRILL

THE COMBINATIONS of turn and trill were indicated in the works of the 18th-century French composers by the superposition of the individual signs. This composite symbol (see Example 36a) which occurs in some of the manuscript sources of Bach's organ works,[6] has been rejected by modern editors in favor of one given by Bach in his table (Example 36b). The ornament appears in Bach's works both with[7] and without[8] termination. The termination is either indicated by a vertical stroke through the end of

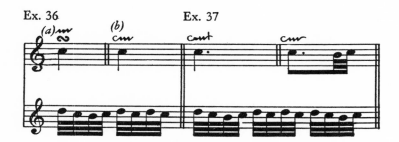

Ex. 36   Ex. 37

the wavy line, or else it is written out in notes (see Example 37). It is obvious that if the ornament is to last longer than it does in the illustrations in Example 37, the trill element only (i.e.,

[5] Examples of the sign for trill and mordent: *Wir danken dir* (Peters V, No. 56; *Orgelbüchlein*), m. 3; *Jesu, meine Zuversicht* (Peters V, Anhang, No. 2), m. 2.

[6] E.g., in the manuscript known as the 'Möllersche Handschrift' (Bibl. Wolfheim, Berlin) which is in the handwriting of Bach's friend and relative, Johann Gottlieb Walther.

[7] E.g., *Ach wie nichtig* (Peters V, No. 1; *Orgelbüchlein*), last measure; Pastorale, III, m. 11; *Allein Gott* (Peters VI, No. 9), mm. 8 and 11; id. second section, m. 11; Sonata III, *Vivace*, m. 85.

[8] E.g., *Allein Gott* (Peters VI, No. 8), mm. 22 and 33; *Komm', heiliger Geist* (Peters VII, No. 37), m. 15. See Ex. 39.

the second group of thirty-second notes) should be repeated, not the turn or the termination.

THE APPOGGIATURA FROM BELOW AND TRILL

SINCE this ornament begins with an appoggiatura from below the main note, the opening figure is, strictly speaking, a double appoggiatura (*Schleifer*) to the upper accessory, which is the initial note of the trill. The somewhat equivocal nature of this

Ex. 38

beginning (which might be construed as an inverted turn, had any such ornament existed at the time of Bach) doubtless accounts

for the fact that it was indicated sometimes by two,[9] sometimes
by three[10] tiny notes prefixed to the main note. The combination,
like the foregoing, was used by Bach both with[11] and without[12]
termination. Example 38 shows the many possible ways of indicat-
ing this ornament in the score, according to whether the initial
figure, the termination, both or neither, are written out in notes.
Obviously, in spite of all these signs, there are only *two* ways of
performing the ornament.

Ex. 39

An expedient that is helpful in recognizing the various types
of combined ornaments at sight is to remember that the symbol
is a graphic representation of the course of the ornamental melody. If the hooked line at the beginning of the sign starts from
above and descends before merging into the wavy line, then the

[9] Cf. Fugue in C major (Schirmer III, No. I), penultimate measure.
[10] As in the last movement of the Third (Vivaldi) Concerto (Schirmer V,
No. III), m. 92.
[11] E.g., *Wenn wir in höchsten Nöthen sein* (Peters V, No. 51; *Orgelbüchlein*,
m. 5; Fughetta super: *Wir glauben all' an einen Gott* (Peters VII, No. 61),
mm. 1, 2, etc.; *Allein Gott* (Peters VI, No. 8), m. 17; *Das alte Jahr vergangen ist
(Orgelbüchlein)*, m. 10; *O Lamm Gottes unschuldig* (Peters VII, No. 48), m. 11;
Nun komm', der Heiden Heiland (Peters VII, No. 46), m. 18.
[12] E.g., *Allein Gott* (Peters VI, No. 8), m. 33.

ornament starts with an appoggiatura from *above*. If, on the other hand, the hook starts at the bottom and rises, the ornament begins with an appoggiatura from *below*. The only anomaly is the sign for the turn itself, which proceeds in a direction opposite to that which one would expect.

The graphic aspect of these symbols is illustrated in Example 39, which shows the entrance of the chorale melody in *Komm', heiliger Geist, Herre Gott* as Bach embellished it with several signs for composite ornaments in succession.

Conclusion

AT THIS point the recapitulation of certain broad principles derived from the analysis of the individual ornamental forms may prove useful to the reader. The most far-reaching of these is the maxim that, in the last analysis, all the ornaments found in Bach's music may be reduced to two basic elements—the appoggiatura and the mordent. The appoggiatura, whether from above or from below, represents the harmonic, dissonant, expressive element or ornamentation; the oscillation between the main note and its lower neighbor, on the other hand, represents the purely melodic, decorative aspect. In Bach's music these two kernels are amplified, reiterated, put together in a multitude of combinations, and fitted into innumerable rhythmic patterns. Simple as are the actual constituents of this ornamentation, their artistic arrangement, multiplication, and juxtaposition give rise to an infinite variety of outward forms, each of which is adapted to fulfill its own specific function.

The first task that presents itself to the performer is that of recognizing these functions in individual cases. Wherever an ornament appears as some variety of trill (i.e., amplified appoggiatura) the executant should look first to the harmony of the passage in question. Once the dissonant element is located, he should concern himself with the best method of bringing it effectively into relief. Sometimes this may be done by a sharp, quick attack[1]—more often (particularly in organ playing) the best

---

[1] As in the case of a short trill superimposed on the first note of a mordent. See the examples cited in footnote 3, Chapter V.

expedient is to dwell somewhat upon the dissonance itself. In either case, there should never be too great a discrepancy between the rhythm of the ornament and that of the melody surrounding it—the trill should not stick out like a sore finger. This latter principle should also be observed in dealing with those ornaments which partake of the nature of the mordent. For, while the chief duty of the mordent is, indeed, to heighten melodic activity, this increased activity should not be so sudden as to cause a shock or to provoke the sensation of nervousness or undue agitation. The melodic adornment which is the mordent in Bach's music is rather akin to the *cantabile* of a virtuoso singer than it is to the 'bite' with which the ornament was associated by 16th-century musicians. The best way to attain this *cantabile* is undoubtedly to keep oneself strictly within the rhythmic scheme presented by the composer; use note-values twice (or, in slow tempi, four times) as short as the prevailing rapid notes of the piece; divide them neatly into groups which coincide with the subdivisions of the beat, and the rhythm will flow with uninterrupted smoothness through the ornamented passage.

It may seem to some readers that these general principles of execution have been reiterated with supererogatory insistence. If this is so, it is only because the writer feels that these principles are even more important, for the proper expression of Bach's ornaments, than the actual notes that are played. We have seen, on several occasions, that it is possible to add or subtract notes, or even to substitute one ornament for another, without altering the basic expression of the passage in the slightest. But let the performer anticipate the beat by a single sixty-fourth note, pass over an appoggiatura without sufficient emphasis, play a trill too hurriedly or unrhythmically, and not only is the purpose of the single ornament defeated but the meaning of Bach's entire phrase is falsified.